THE WEST IS CALLING

Imagining British Columbia

BY SARAH N. HARVEY & LESLIE BUFFAM

ILLUSTRATED BY DIANNA BONDER

ORCA BOOK PUBLISHERS

Smoke from longhouse fires shrouds the totems. A whale leaps, rocking the canoes.

Ice water over
jagged rocks. The men are cold.
The west is calling.

Oaks and blue lilies
make way for fences and roads.
Flags salute the wind.

Pebbles in water
glitter. With each bright nugget
the town comes alive.

Deep in the cold earth
ponies whinny in the dark.
A canary sings.

They have come by sea
to lay the great steel ribbon
across the harsh land.

No longer silent,
the forest yields to the saws.
Nests are not safe now.

The Laughing One dreams of ancient forests. Woo sits, watching the brush strokes.

Millions of salmon
in hundreds of boats. Dinner
will be ready soon.

The town has vanished.
Walls hold the dark water back,
but the lights shine on.

BENNETT
DAM
·VIEWPOINT·

25¢

The dogs wear booties
to race across ice and snow.
Northern lights dazzle.

An invitation
to the whole world: Visit us.
C'est magnifique!

Protect what is left.
Wolves howl and trees stand silent.
The spirit bear lives.

Longhouses rise up
above the rocky shore. Look.
Some things do not change.

HISTORICAL NOTES

1. HAIDA VILLAGE—PRE-CONTACT

For more than 6000 years, Haida Gwaii, the islands off the northwest coast of British Columbia, has been home to the Haida people, a complex society with a rich artistic tradition. The Haida were known as fierce warriors and expert fishermen, hunters and woodworkers. Shellfish, cod, salmon and halibut were plentiful and an essential part of their diet. The native red cedar provided clothing, shelter, utensils and transportation.

2. ALEXANDER MACKENZIE—1790s

Alexander Mackenzie, a North West Company fur trader, worked tirelessly to find an overland route to the Pacific Ocean. With one canoe and 3000 pounds of supplies, Mackenzie and nine other men spent seventy-two days paddling, poling and hauling their canoe through harsh terrain. On July 22, 1793, Mackenzie and his companions reached the Pacific Ocean at North Bentinck Arm, but he had not found a viable route for the fur trade.

3. FOUNDING OF FORT VICTORIA—1840s

In 1842, the Hudson's Bay Company sent James Douglas to Vancouver Island to search for a safe location for its northwest fur trading headquarters. Douglas chose a site at the southern tip of Vancouver Island. He described the place as "a perfect Eden, in the midst of the dreary wilderness of the Northwest coast." Construction of the fort began in 1843, with the help of the Songhees people who lived in two nearby villages.

4. THE GOLD RUSH—1850s-1860s

In 1857, natives living where the Thompson and Fraser rivers meet discovered gold, launching a gold rush that changed the face of the colony. Over 30,000 men and women flocked to the area in search of easy wealth. This invasion led, in 1858, to the creation of the colony of British Columbia. The search for gold continued throughout the 1860s and moved north into the Cariboo, where the town of Barkerville sprang up to meet the needs of the miners.

5. COAL MINING ON VANCOUVER ISLAND—LATE 1870s

In 1852, a native named Coal Tyee shared his knowledge of Nanaimo's coal seam with the Hudson's Bay Company. Coal was in great demand, and experienced miners were brought in to attack the rich seams of "black gold." Coal mining was extremely hard and dangerous work; miners, including boys as young as eight, worked by hand, deep underground, with only the light of small open lamps.

6. BUILDING THE CANADIAN PACIFIC RAILWAY—1880s

In 1871, the promise of a national railway persuaded British Columbians to join Canada. When construction began in 1880, thousands of workers laboured with picks and shovels to carve the railway through the mountains and canyons of the interior. Many lives were lost to rockslides, dynamite blasts and drowning. On November 7, 1885, Donald Smith, the CPR's president, drove the last spike at Craigellachie, at the western entrance to Eagle Pass.

7. LOGGING ON THE BC COAST—1900s

By the 1900s, BC's logging industry was growing rapidly, fueled by the expansion of the railways and the building boom in the Prairie provinces. What had begun as a handlogging operation, aided by animals, quickly became mechanized. Highriggers, buckers, chokermen, donkey punchers and whistle punks replaced handloggers. With the machines came speed and the ability to log vast areas of forest.

8. EMILY CARR—1920s

Emily Carr (1871–1945) had to wait until the late 1920s to have her talent as a painter of the landscapes and native cultures of the Pacific Coast recognized. An invitation to exhibit with the Group of Seven meant she no longer had to earn her living as a dog breeder and boarding house keeper. To the Nuu-chah-nulth, whose culture she captured so powerfully, she was Klee Wyck ("the laughing one"); to the Group of Seven, she was the "Mother of Modern Arts."

9. FISH CANNING INDUSTRY—1940s

By the 1870s, the salmon canning industry was well established at the mouth of the Fraser River. What began as a labour-intensive enterprise, with native and Chinese workers in the canneries, over time became a highly mechanized one where three could do the work of thirty. By the early 1900s, Japanese immigrants, both men and women, dominated the fishing and canning industries, creating a strong Japanese community in the Steveston/Richmond area.

10. PEACE RIVER (BENNETT) DAM—1960s

By the 1950s, demand for British Columbia's natural resources provided revenues for projects that focused on transportation, power and industrial growth. The largest of the power projects was the Peace River (later renamed Bennett) Dam. By 1967, there was a 649-square-mile lake behind a four-hundred-foot-tall earth-filled dam. While the dam generated an enormous amount of cheap electricity, the lake behind it destroyed the small town of Finlay Forks.

11. THE NORTH—1970s

Northern British Columbia occupies more than half the province. Premier W.A.C. Bennett's (1952–1972) "northern vision" led to the opening up of this vast area and to the development of its natural resources. Fort Nelson is home to both the largest gas-processing plant in North America and the Canadian Open Dog Sled Races. As the area became more accessible, its spectacular landscapes and vast assortment of wildlife began to attract a growing number of visitors.

12. EXPO 86—1980s

At a time when a worldwide recession reduced the demand for the province's natural resources, there was one bright spot for British Columbians. Expo 86, a world's fair focusing on transportation and communication, helped Vancouver celebrate its centennial. Between May 2 and October 13, 1986, there were over twenty-two million visitors to the site. Expo 86 put Vancouver on the international map and helped make it the important tourist destination it is today.

13. GREAT BEAR RAINFOREST—1990s–2000s

By the 1980s, it had become clear that the province's resources were not endless. Clear-cut logging in the old-growth rainforest of Clayoquot Sound sparked massive protests and brought about some change. The continued focus on the protection of BC's coastal temperate rainforests led to the establishment, in 2006, of the Great Bear Rainforest Agreement, a work-in-progress that has offered some protection to one of the world's most endangered ecosystems.

14. THE TSESHAHT FIRST NATION—2008

The province's First Nations have long expressed anger and concern about the loss of traditional lands and repeatedly pressed their claims for redress. In the 1990s, as First Nations gained in both numbers and confidence, the provincial government acknowledged that some form of settlement must be reached. A six-step treaty process was initiated. Though progress remains slow, many First Nations have begun rebuilding their communities.

SEEK AND FIND!

1   drying rack for salmon, totem pole, longhouse, killer whale, salmon, seal, eagle, western red cedar, children, feather

2   voyageur, native guide, children, moose, eagle, rabbit, common merganser, fish, great horned owl, lodgepole pine, Indian paintbrush

3   James Douglas, Hudson's Bay Company ship *Beaver*, Garry oak, camas lily, stockade fence, surveyor's tent, saw, round shovel, flat shovel, canoe, children, robin, Red Ensign flag

4   pack mule, pack horse, dog, children, crow, Steller's jay, hurdy-gurdy girl, miner, hoop, gold, pick, gold pan

5   pit pony, hand pick, headlamp, miner's lamp, caged canary, tea and sugar tins, children, black bear, Vancouver Island marmot, arbutus tree, coal

6   cook tent, mule, railroad tie, dog, picture of child, mallet, shovel, hand pick, tree stump, hat

7   steam donkey, axe, bucking saw, jack, Sitka spruce, varied thrush nest, broken egg, firewood, children

8   Emily Carr, the Elephant (caravan), bob-tailed sheepdog, Woo (monkey), parrot, cedar, fir, butterfly, wild rose, palette, paintbrush, canvas, children

9   fishboat, corkline, net, children, salmon, gull, mooring buoy, sailboat, piling, wharf, fishknife

10   eagle, hawk, grizzly bear with cub, bird, tree, camera, bandana, sunglasses, backpack, children, viewfinder

11   snowshoes, booties, children, moose, raccoon, fox, rabbit, sled dog, cross-country skier, ice skater, toque, sled, skis and poles

12   Expo Ernie, Swatch, Expo Centre, Expo banner, balloon, gull, mountain, children, Expo T-shirt, gondola

13   mew gull, great horned owl, wolf, Kermode bear and cub, porcupine, rabbit, frog, children, tent, fern, Sitka spruce

14   longhouse, boat, children, sea otter, brush, sieve, mural, totem pole, basket, pottery, dog, tattoo

How many can you find?

For Leslie—SH

For Katie and Bonar—LB

To Nico and Ekko and all the children who have shared their smiles throughout our rich history—DB

Text copyright © 2008 Sarah N. Harvey and Leslie Buffam
Illustrations copyright © 2008 Dianna Bonder

Library and Archives Canada Cataloguing in Publication

Harvey, Sarah N., 1950-
The West is calling / Sarah N. Harvey & Leslie Buffam; illustrated by Dianna Bonder.

ISBN 978-1-55143-936-5

1. British Columbia--History--Juvenile poetry. 2. Haiku, Canadian (English). 3. Children's poetry, Canadian (English). I. Buffam, Leslie II. Bonder, Dianna, 1970- III. Title.

PS8615.A764W48 2008   jC811'.6   C2008-902686-1

First published in the United States, 2008
Library of Congress Control Number: 2008927291

Summary: A celebration in haiku and illustration of 150 years of British Columbian history.

Orca Book Publishers gratefully acknowledges the support for its publishing programs provided by the following agencies: the Government of Canada through the Book Publishing Industry Development Program and the Canada Council for the Arts, and the Province of British Columbia through the BC Arts Council and the Book Publishing Tax Credit.

Cover artwork by Dianna Bonder
Design by Teresa Bubela
Author photo by Dayle Sutherland

ORCA BOOK PUBLISHERS   ORCA BOOK PUBLISHERS
PO Box 5626, STN. B   PO Box 468
VICTORIA, BC CANADA   CUSTER, WA USA
V8R 6S4   98240-0468

www.orcabook.com
Printed and bound in China.
11 10 09 08 • 4 3 2 1